# I SPY EASTER

This Book Belongs To

_____

_____

_____

D1397495

# I-SPY with my little eye someting starting with......

# I-SPY with my little eye someting starting with......

**B**

Is for......

BUNNY

# I-SPY with my little eye someting starting with......

C

Is for......

CHICKEN

# I-SPY with my little eye someting starting with......

D Is for......

DINOSAUR

# I-SPY with my little eye someting starting with......

E Is for......

ELEPHANT

# I-SPY with my little eye someting starting with......

# F

Is for......

FOX

# I-SPY with my little eye someting starting with......

Is for......

GNOME

# I-SPY with my little eye someting starting with......

**Is for......**

**HIPPO**

# I-SPY with my little eye someting starting with.......

Is for......

INSECT

# I-SPY with my little eye someting starting with.......

J

Is for......

JESUS

# I-SPY with my little eye someting starting with......

K

Is for......

KOALA

# I-SPY with my little eye someting starting with......

Is for......

LION

# I-SPY with my little eye someting starting with......

# M
## Is for......
# MONKEY

# I-SPY with my little eye someting starting with......

Is for......

NEST

# I-SPY with my little eye someting starting with......

OWL

# I-SPY with my little eye someting starting with......

**P**

Is for......

**POLAR BEAR**

# I-SPY with my little eye someting starting with......

Is for......

QUEEN BEE

# I-SPY with my little eye someting starting with......

**R**

Is for......

RABBIT

# I-SPY with my little eye someting starting with......

# I-SPY with my little eye someting starting with......

**T**

Is for......

**TURTLE**

# I-SPY with my little eye someting starting with......

Is for......

UNICORN

# I-SPY with my little eye someting starting with......

**V** Is for......

**VASE**

# I-SPY with my little eye someting starting with......

Is for......

WATERMELON

# I-SPY with my little eye someting starting with.......

Is for......

XYLOPHONE

# I-SPY with my little eye someting starting with......

Y

Is for......

YO YO

# I-SPY with my little eye someting starting with......

ZEBRA

Made in the USA
Middletown, DE
03 April 2022

63576992R00031